I wish I had had access to these materials when I was in eighth grade. There is nothing more important than empowering our young people to value their own individuality, which encourages them to become full participating members of our society. They are our future, and LifeBound has the ability to empower them!

—*Kate Eaton*
HABITAT FOR HUMANITY INTERNATIONAL

Like most of us, teens need help getting in touch with their feelings. I was most impressed with the chapter on extreme emotions, such as anger and anxiety, which can throw students into crisis and eventually lead to depression. This book also can help students better understand other people's feelings and other important aspects of maturity.

—*Mildred McKelvin*
RETIRED CHICAGO HIGH SCHOOL TEACHER

People Smarts can help students recognize that their emotional make-up and the challenges they may face emotionally are very common. Teens will find the practical suggestions on how to deal with certain emotions extremely helpful.

—*Angela Steinhart*
PARENT OF MIDDLE SCHOOL STUDENT

people
smarts
FOR
teenagers

CAROL CARTER

LifeBound
DENVER, COLORADO

Publisher: Carol Carter
Managing Editor: Dylan Lewis
Developmental Editor: Cynthia Nordberg
Production: Holcomb Hathaway
Cover and Interior Design: Aerocraft Charter Art Service
Printing and Binding: Data Reproductions

LifeBound
1530 High Street
Denver, Colorado 80218
www.lifebound.com

ISBN 10: 0–9742044–4–7
ISBN 13: 978–0–9742044–4–4

10 9 8 7 6 5 4 3 2 1

Printed in the United States of America.

CONTENTS

Managing Strong Emotions   25

Self-Motivation   39

Developing Social Skills   53

Stress   67

PREFACE

The teen years are fraught with emotional ups and downs. Students often don't know why they feel they way they do and many wonder if their feelings are normal. Some teens report the gnawing perception that no one understands them, and they may act out this frustration with anti-social behavior that masks the underlying issues. Left unresolved, these intense and lonely feelings can lead to adolescent depression and ultimately dissatisfaction later in life.

This book will be a refreshing antidote to the emotional upheaval that many teens face, as well as support for those teens who are thriving. Throughout these chapters, we show students how to manage their emotions in life-enriching ways, and we encourage them to develop a compassionate heart, which is one of the shining tenets of emotional intelligence. In the process, we alert teens to the common pitfalls on the road to becoming emotionally mature, and we reveal the inextricable link between emotional well-being and life success. LifeBound's dedication to the academic and emotional development of today's young people has driven this publication. We hope this book will offer constructive help to readers experiencing the challenges common to teen years.

ACKNOWLEDGMENTS

'd like to take the time to recognize the names of the people who contributed to this project.

Thank you to the many teachers who will be reinforcing these positive messages in their classrooms, including: Mildred McKelvin, Lisette Perez, and Janet Kraft.

Without input from parents, LifeBound could never tailor our publications to their children. So, thank you Mary Fields, Dennis McMahan, Tim Nordberg, and Angie Steinhart.

Of course, thank you to the many students who contributed to the completion of this project, namely: Andrew Steinhart, Darius Logan, Nalisha Logan, Yael Sharon, and Rebekah Fields.

Special thanks to the following people for their dedication in completing this publication:

Dylan Lewis, our managing editor, who was thorough in working with all the people whose insights produced this book, and who also created exercises that will encourage students to think and to discover their full potential; Cynthia Nordberg, our developmental editor, who created the stories that open every chapter and worked diligently to get feedback and comments from students and parents; Lissa Kate Morhorski, who was a great help in the final editing stages; Vijali Brown, for her input and feedback and her fabulous promotional skills; Megan Walker, for her ideas on stories and profiles that fill this book; Jennifer Amanda Keller, for her "Mean Girls" story depicting the difficult topic of bullying; Amy Wojciak, who learned to love writing and researching the profiles in addition to her strong marketing background; and Brian Landever, whose reviewers helped us put the final touches on the last draft. Thanks for all of your hard work, dedication, and perseverance.

Carol Carter

people
smarts

FOR TEENAGERS

CHAPTER ONE

defining emotional intelligence

ew York City resident Omar Eduardo Rivera, a blind computer technician, was at his desk with his guide dog "Dorado" on the 71st floor of the north tower of the World Trade Center when a hijacked airplane struck the building twenty-five floors above him. Rivera heard crashing glass, and smoke began to fill the room.

He unleashed Dorado, a four-year-old Labrador Retriever, so the dog could escape. "I hoped he would be able to quickly run down the stairs without me and get to safety," explained Rivera. "I thought he'd be so scared he'd run. Everything was in chaos and everyone was rushing down the stairs."

Dorado disappeared into a throng of people, and Rivera was resigned to die. Suddenly he felt a familiar fuzzy nose at his knee—Dorado had returned! The faithful friend then guided Rivera down seventy flights of stairs and out onto the street just before the building collapsed.

"It was then I knew for certain he loved me just as much as I loved him. He was prepared to die in the hope he might save my life," Rivera reported.*

As this story illustrates, animals often show high degrees of what researchers call *emotional intelligence*. In this case, Dorado's empathy actually saved the life of his human companion. Amazing accounts of animal behavior throughout the earthquake and tsunami in southeast Asia in December 2004 also testify to this intuitive aspect of intelligence. For example, elephants were reported to have demonstrated agitation and anxiety minutes before the earthquake hit. They also showed heroic deeds of rescue in the aftermath, using their strong trunks to pull people to safety.

Human beings also have a unique capability to sense danger, as well as other warning signs, an ability that some people call a "sixth sense." Just as our five senses help us perceive the world around us in tangible ways, so do our feelings help us pick up on important clues about ourselves and other people.

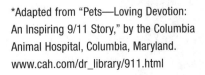

Having emotional intelligence is like having an antenna that receives all kinds of signals, alerting us to things that are potentially helpful or hurtful. Sometimes our antenna signals to us that something is pleasurable. Being with our friends, for instance, makes us feel good. Other times our emotional radar tells us that something is wrong. For instance, someone puts us down, and that makes

*Adapted from "Pets—Loving Devotion: An Inspiring 9/11 Story," by the Columbia Animal Hospital, Columbia, Maryland. www.cah.com/dr_library/911.html

us feel bad. Emotional intelligence is a vital sense organ that helps us understand the feeling side of life. It's important that we learn to understand our feelings because we often act out the way we feel, which can create all kinds of positive and negative effects in our lives.

For instance, have you ever been so angry that you thought you might explode yet you managed to gain self-control before going off? Have you ever tried to talk to someone who gave you the cold shoulder and wondered what might have happened that caused him or her to respond this way? Have you ever done something that you felt was wrong and tried to figure out why you did it? If you answered "yes" to any of these questions, then you were practicing emotional intelligence. Emotionally intelligent people often have the ability to understand their own feelings as well as the feelings of others.

Daniel Goleman, a psychologist, was one of the first people to use the term "emotional intelligence." He defines emotional intelligence as having self-awareness. He says you are self-aware when you recognize your own feelings, as well as those of others; when you know if thoughts and feelings are ruling your decisions; and when you see a link between those thoughts and feelings. Another part of emotional intelligence is learning how to manage three common human emotions: anxiety, anger, and sadness. Emotional

FRIDA KAHLO

World-Renowned Modern Artist

As a child, Frida Kahlo of Mexico City contracted polio, which caused her right leg to be much thinner than the other. In high school, she was labeled as a "tomboy full of mischief" and became the ringleader of a rebellious group of mainly boys. It was also in high school that Frida first came in contact with her future husband, the famous Mexican muralist Diego Rivera. He was commissioned to paint a mural in the school's auditorium.

On September 17, 1925, at about age 18, Frida Kahlo was in a serious bus accident that broke her spinal column. For a month, she was forced to stay flat on her back, encased in a plaster body cast. Although she was able to walk after the accident, for the remainder of her life she experienced almost unbearable physical pain and exhaustion. She often had to be hospitalized for long periods of time, and she underwent 30 operations during her lifetime.

Kahlo's emotional strength helped her face the relentless pain. To relieve the boredom of being in bed so much she began painting, and art became her lifelong passion. "I paint self-portraits because I am so often alone, because I am the person I know best," she said.

Like many artists, Kahlo expressed her emotions on canvas. She painted her anger and hurt over the physical suffering she endured as a result of the accident. At her last art exhibition in Mexico, Frida told reporters, "I am not sick. I am broken. But I am happy as long as I can paint."

Adapted from *Biography of Frida Kahlo,*
http://members.aol.com/fridanet/fridabio.htm

intelligence also includes taking responsibility for your decisions and actions, as well as following through on commitments you've made.

Five elements make up emotional intelligence. We will examine these one at a time in the rest of this book:

- Self-awareness
- Managing strong emotions
- Self-motivation
- Empathy
- Managing relationships

Q Versus IQ

No doubt you've heard about IQ (intelligence quotient), and you can take some tests that try to determine how book smart you are. Well, you can think of EQ (emotional quotient) in a similar way. A person's emotional quotient is a way of measuring "people smarts," which is the ability to interact and relate well to others. EQ is an extremely valuable and practical ability to have. People who develop their EQ do better in school, in their professions, and in their lives. After all, we talk to people and listen to people all day long. If we learn to be more understanding of the thoughts and emotions of others, we can know more about ourselves and, in turn, live a happier and more satisfying life.

exercise 1.1

RECOGNIZING EMOTIONS

Using illustrations in magazines of different faces, identify the emotion the person in the picture is feeling.

_____

_____

_____

_____

_____

_____

exercise 1.2

RECOGNIZING EMOTIONS

Write five words that are used to describe certain emotions. For example, "aggravated" is what a teacher feels when students talk during class. Then describe what it is like to feel "aggravated."

1. _____

_____

_____

_____

_____

2. _____

_____

_____

_____

_____

_____

_____

3. _____

_____

_____

_____

_____

_____

_____

4. _____

_____

_____

_____

_____

_____

_____

5. _____

_____

_____

_____

_____

_____

_____

hy Do You Need EI (Emotional Intelligence)?

In science class you've learned about "survival of the fittest" and how it relates to the animal kingdom. People also use survival skills. Think about the reality TV shows you may have watched. The person who survives or who doesn't get kicked off the island isn't always the one who's physically strongest or even the most brilliant. The person who survives is the one who can get along with the rest of the group and who doesn't freak out when there's a problem.

To survive school and ultimately life, you'll need more than book smarts. Students can have a high IQ and still flunk out in other areas of life because they don't have the coping skills or social savvy they need to survive. Knowing how to manage your emotions and how to relate to other people are keys to lasting success. The rest of this book will show you why.

motional Intelligence Assessment

Circle the answer that fits you best.

1. You have just found out that you got an A on the first exam of the semester. What do you do?

   a. Decide not to study for the next exam since you've done so well.

   b. Study a little bit, but you know that even if you get a C, your average will still be a B.

   c. Study with someone who didn't do well on the first exam, so you can help him or her.

   d. Study alone for hours to make sure you keep up your A average.

2. You've just broken your father's windshield with a baseball. What do you do?

   a. Deny that you had anything to do with it.

   b. Tell your Dad that although the window is broken, he needed a new one anyway.

   c. Tell him what happened and apologize.

   d. Make up a story how it was your best friend's fault and that you shouldn't be punished.

3. A bully in your gym class has just stolen your lunch. What do you do?

   a. Challenge him to a fight after school.

   b. Punch him during class, take your lunch back, and hope he doesn't kill you.

   c. Try to talk him into giving your lunch back.

   d. Tell the teacher and hope the bully isn't waiting for you after school.

4. Your friends are going to a big Halloween party, but you have homework to do. What do you do?

   a. Go to the party and hope you can finish your homework before class on Monday.

   b. Finish some of your homework and then go to the party later.

   c. Call your teacher and ask for an extension on Monday's due date.

   d. Stay home and finish your homework.

Review your answers to these questions and compare them to what you've learned in this chapter. Remember that there are no right answers, nor are there any wrong answers.

show what you know

1. What is emotional intelligence? Define it.

_____

_____

_____

_____

_____

_____

_____

_____

2. In what ways have animals demonstrated emotional intelligence?

_____

_____

_____

_____

_____

_____

_____

3. Who is Frida Kahlo?

_____

_____

_____

_____

_____

_____

_____

keeping your journal

How can emotional intelligence help you in school and in life?

CHAPTER TWO

self-awareness

U nderstanding Who You Are

Candace was just two years old and could hardly breathe. "My mother said that when the doctors told her I had asthma, she didn't know how life-threatening it could be," Candace says now. From the time she was little, every time Candace caught a simple cold, she wound up in the intensive care unit of the hospital with needles in her arms and an oxygen mask covering her face. She remembers spending many holidays in the hospital, because holidays were when her cousins would come over and often she'd catch a cold from them and become deathly ill.

When Candace was seven years old, doctors told her parents that her best hope for recovery was long-term treatment at an asthma research institute in Denver, Colorado. At the hospital were doctors from all over the world who specialized in helping kids with asthma. The hard part for Candace and

her parents, though, was that she would have to live there for up to two years without her family. One of the problems that kids who have a serious illness experience is that parents and other caregivers tend to hover over them and not allow them to try new things. The clinic helps children learn how to cope with their asthma and to become more independent.

At the age of eight, Candace became a patient at the Children's Asthma Research Institute and Hospital. "A new world opened to me there," explains Candace. "I attended school for the first time as a third grader (until then I had been home schooled), and the house moms took us to do fun things that I hadn't been able to do before, like swimming and hiking in the mountains. My newfound freedom left little time for homesickness, but sometimes, especially at night, waves of it would come. Then, when our dormitory was quiet, I would cry in my pillow," Candace says.

Candace's two-year stay at the clinic greatly improved her health, and today she is almost asthma-free. Her experience at the institute also taught her a lot about herself and the world at large. For example, Candace discovered that she likes to write. Early on she started keeping a journal as a way to vent her feelings. If she was feeling lonely or overwhelmed, she would write it down and it would help her feel better. She also found out that by simply smiling and saying "hi," she could make friends easily. "I learned how to take care of myself and how to not be afraid of change, but to see new people and new experiences as a way to enjoy life more and learn more about myself," says Candace.

What Is Self-Awareness?

Of the five parts of emotional intelligence, it is important to learn about self-awareness first because it is foundational to emotional health. We are self-aware when we recognize a feeling or an emotion. This type of recognition is the basis for emotional intelligence. When you understand your feelings, you can usually better understand why you behave the way you do in a certain situation and why you make the decisions you make. As you decide about school, work, or other parts of your life, you will find that knowing *why* you feel the way you do will give you greater certainty and confidence that you are making the best decision for you.

Self-awareness occurs not only when we understand what we are feeling, but also when we understand what we do about how we're feeling. Being *self-aware* is like having a part of your brain that manages your emotions. In people who are self-aware, this voice acts as a neutral voice of reason. For example, if you are becoming angry at any given situation, the self-aware portion of your brain chimes in to tell you why you are feeling angry and may encourage your angry mind to relax and to think about the consequences of your anger.

Reading Your Emotions

It is important to recognize that someone who is unaware of his or her thoughts and feelings may not have developed a full sense of self-awareness. The full sense of self-awareness comes when someone is able to control negative actions that may result from unpleasant emotions. This is not to say that anger is the only emotion worthy of discussion. Recognizing and determining proper actions as a result of joy and happiness, or any other emotions, are equally important for a healthy emotional state.

CHRIS EYRE

Native American Director and Film Producer

Chris Eyre, who is part Cheyenne and part Arapaho, is highly self-aware, which is why he only makes movies that feel right to him personally. His interest in film making began in high school when he got involved in landscape photography. In an interview with *Native Peoples Magazine* Eyre said, "You're mesmerized by certain images as a child, and I search for that image when I make a movie. If I'm moved by the story, that's when I want to do it."

Eyre's most recent film, *A Thousand Roads,* is being shown at the Smithsonian's National Museum of the American Indian in Washington, D.C. The film is about four American Indians living in Peru, New York City, the Navajo Nation in New Mexico, and Alaska and the role their heritage plays in their lives. Parts of the film were shot in minus-40-degree weather in Alaska.

American Indian people have never "evolved in front of the camera," Eyre said in the interview with *Native Peoples Magazine.* "We've come all this way and native people are still the same. They are either portrayed as 'spiritually endowed' or as 'savage antagonists.' I truly believe that movies can change our view of the world and how we see other people."

Adapted from *Native Peoples Magazine,* March/April 2002, "A Conversation with Chris Eyre," by Delphine Red Shirt, www.native peoples.com/np_mar_apr02/ma02-article1/ma02-article.html

exercise 2.1

BECOMING SELF-AWARE

Write down an experience you have had where you couldn't explain the emotions you were feeling at the time, maybe because you felt confused or you hadn't faced a situation like this ever before. What do you understand about that issue now that you didn't understand then?

Imagine not being able to recognize any type of emotion. You cry when you see a sad movie, cheer at a football game, and shriek when you see a scary movie, but you really have no idea why. There are people out there like that. They react to the emotion but have no idea why they feel the way they do. These types of people have a condition called *alexithymia*. These people cannot put their feelings into words.

John Mayer, a University of New Hampshire psychologist and a co-formulator of the theory of emotional intelligence, says that self-awareness is being "aware of both our moods and our thoughts about our moods." When we look at our feelings and say, "I shouldn't be feeling this way," we are recognizing our emotions. Furthermore, when we recognize these feelings, we are essentially saying that we wish to understand what we are feeling.

Your Conscious Brain

The emotional part of our brain is aware of things much earlier than our conscious brain is. For example, in one psychological experiment with adults, researchers flashed pictures of snakes for a fraction of a second to people who are afraid of snakes. These people showed the emotional effects of fear—sweating and a rapid heartbeat—before the conscious part of their brain had time to recognize what it was seeing. Based on this research as well as on other experiments, psychologists now say that there is not an equal relationship between our conscious brain and our emotional brain. This is why it is so important to recognize what we are feeling, why we are feeling it, and what we should do about our feelings.

Your Intense Emotions

You may have never thought about this before, but we all feel things with different *intensity*. Every emotion you see other people express may differ from the way you feel. Your degree of happiness when playing with a puppy, for instance, will be different from the person next to you playing with the same puppy. Not only do we feel emotions at different *intensities*, but we also react differently given identical situations.

Sometimes our relationships with our friends and family can be troubling. However, we should be careful to weigh our emotions against the severity of the incident or problem. In other words, it is important to put your feelings in perspective. To put things in perspective means to weigh how you feel against what has happened that caused you to feel that way.

For example, you just got a new pair of jeans that you thought looked really cool in the store. The next day you wear them to school, but your new jeans have turned out to be very uncool. Your friends immediately start a barrage of under-handed remarks, remarks meant to make others laugh at your expense. After a few minutes of ridicule, you are embarrassed and even a little angry with your friends for giving you such grief. Yet you are able to put the situation in perspective by realizing that even though your friends are making fun of your jeans, they aren't making fun of you. Also, you know them well enough to realize that they really mean no harm. They are just having some fun, and it isn't a pattern of how they usually treat you. Your ability to maintain your composure and not get angry with them is a way to measure your emotional intelligence. In this situation, you have realized how you feel about your friends and you decide it's not worth getting worked up about. Plus, you aren't overly concerned about pleasing everybody else. Problem solved.

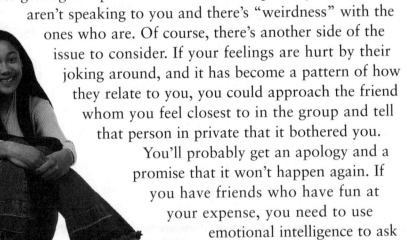

On the other hand, let's say you tell your friends off. You let them know exactly what you think of them for making fun of your jeans. As you walk away, you silently vow never to talk to your so-called friends ever again. The next morning you regret getting so upset because now a couple of your friends aren't speaking to you and there's "weirdness" with the ones who are. Of course, there's another side of the issue to consider. If your feelings are hurt by their joking around, and it has become a pattern of how they relate to you, you could approach the friend whom you feel closest to in the group and tell that person in private that it bothered you. You'll probably get an apology and a promise that it won't happen again. If you have friends who have fun at your expense, you need to use emotional intelligence to ask yourself whether these are the kinds of friends you really want in the first place.

Here are a few activities that promote self-awareness:

- Asking questions
- Journaling
- Transforming the past
- Holding your vision for what's possible

exercise 2.2

BECOMING SELF-AWARE

This exercise was designed by Suzanne Miller, a psychologist at Temple University, to determine whether people in stressful situations tend to be hyperaware, noticing everything that happens, or distracted so as not to think about the anxiety the predicament is causing.

Imagine you are in an airplane and the pilot's voice comes over the intercom saying, "Please buckle your seat belt. We'll be experiencing turbulence as we approach Chicago." Outside the plane window you can see lightning, and thunder rocks the plane. An oxygen mask falls from above your seat, and you feel weightless as the plane descends into the airport. How do you imagine you would react at this point?

_____

_____

_____

_____

_____

_____

_____

_____

_____

_____

_____

_____

_____

_____

_____

_____

_____

Stranger Danger

As a little kid you learned about "stranger danger." Your parents told you, "Never talk to strangers or take candy from somebody you don't know." This was great advice. Now, what if that stranger is yourself? If you think about it, not understanding why you do what you do and why you feel what you feel is like going through your life with a stranger's mind. How do you make wise decisions and choices if you don't understand why you want what you want? It's a difficult and chaotic way to live, never knowing what this stranger is going to do next.

Questions can help you become more self-aware. Are you where you live? Are you your hobbies? Are you what you look like? Your answers to these questions are only reflections of who you are to the outside world. But it's just that, a reflection of your inner self. To go below the surface, the questions need to be more meaningful.

- With what type of people do I enjoy spending time?
- Why don't I like being made fun of?
- What do I think is one of the best ideas I've ever had?
- Who am I when no one else is around?

The famous scientist Carl Sagan once said, "We make the world significant by the courage of our questions, and by the depth of our answers." Don't be afraid to ask yourself or other people hard questions. It's cool to be curious!

show what you know

DEMONSTRATE YOUR UNDERSTANDING

1. *What is self-awareness? Define it.*

_____

_____

_____

_____

_____

_____

2. *Who is Chris Eyre?*

_____

_____

_____

_____

_____

_____

3. *Why might some people be unaware of how they feel?*

_____

_____

_____

_____

_____

_____

keeping your journal

GET IN TOUCH WITH HOW YOU FEEL

What are some of your most intense emotions? How can you become more self-aware in order to manage those feelings?

_____

_____

_____

_____

_____

_____

_____

_____

_____

_____

_____

_____

_____

_____

_____

_____

_____

_____

_____

_____

_____

_____

_____

_____

_____

managing strong emotions

S taying in Control

Everyone at school could see Paul had an anger problem. For example, one fall afternoon during recess, Paul's classmate made a comment about him liking a certain girl. In the flash of a second, Paul whirled around and hit his classmate squarely in the mouth, causing the boy's lip to gush blood. Immediately, the teacher on duty and other students ran toward them. Paul was sent to the principal's office and given three days' suspension from school.

That week, Paul's mother made an appointment for him with a counselor who specializes in working with troubled youth. At their first meeting, Paul was mad, as usual. Everything about his body language said, "I don't want to be here." He slouched in his chair, pulled his hooded sweatshirt over his eyes, and folded his arms across his chest. The counselor was not intimidated by Paul's countenance. Instead, he asked him a

simple question, "Paul, what makes you really mad?" Paul began to cry. There were so many things that made him angry that he felt overwhelmed by the question.

After a few sessions with the counselor, Paul began to understand how to control his anger rather than letting it control him. When the counselor asked, "What are some things you can do when you get angry, rather than hit someone or something?" Paul honestly replied, "I don't know." The counselor proceeded to give Paul some ideas: he could walk away from the person taunting him, he could talk to a friend about his feelings, he could exercise, he could write about how he felt at that moment, he could draw or listen to music, and so forth. Paul liked what he was learning. Now he uses some of these ideas, and some of his own (such as playing with his pet lizard "Scales"), to calm down before he does something that will hurt himself or someone else.

Suffering Setbacks

Throughout your life you will suffer setbacks and disappointments. Everyone does. The way you handle these events, however, will greatly affect your ability to recover and learn from them. If you are unable to combat feelings of anxiety, gloom, or irritability, you may almost constantly feel distressed. If you have ever done poorly on a test or while playing sports, then you know what it feels like to be disappointed. It is not unhealthy to have these feelings because they're a natural reaction to your less-than-desired circumstance.

However, if we let disappointment over the last test's grade destroy our motivation to study for the next test, then we let the negative emotions win. Remember what the last chapter said about putting things into perspective? It is easy to get so discouraged about grades, but when you look at the overall situation you'll see that it is only *one* test in *one* class. It's nothing to lose sleep over.

Finding the Balance

When our emotions are extreme, we allow them to manage our lives. For example, a person who is sad most of the time tends to have a negative outlook on life, and that negative personality affects how others see him or her. At the other extreme, a person who acts happy all the time can seem out of touch with reality and even a bit odd. Of course, some situations call for us to be extremely happy or extremely sad, and people who manage their emotions in a healthy way learn to balance sadness with happiness, despair with hope, and so on. Emotionally intelligent people can adjust their emotions according to what's appropriate at the time. So we are happy when something good happens to our friends, and likewise we are sad when they are hurting. We also empathize with ourselves in the same way. We expect our friends to share in our happiness and in our disappointments.

It is important to know that when we manage our emotions we are not always trying to suppress them. Instead, we are attempting to find a healthy balance between our emotional brain and our logical brain. When we attempt to mute our

ERIK WEIHENMAYER
Extreme Adventurist and Professional Mountain Climber

Imagine for a minute that you are blind. While you might be able to make it around your house in the dark, picture what it would be like trying to climb a mountain. As you experienced the sensation of being high up without sight, can you imagine the fear that could overtake you? What kind of determination would a person need to keep climbing?

On May 25, 2001, Erik Weihenmayer, age 34, overcame his fears and became the first blind climber to reach Mt. Everest, the world's tallest peak at 29,035 feet. It was a climb that was later designated as one of "Sports Best" by *Time* magazine. Later he was invited to meet the president of the United States and to scale the rock wall of the Matterhorn ride with Mickey Mouse at Disneyland.

In his book, *Touch the Top of the World: A Blind Man's Journey to Climb Farther than the Eye Can See,* Weihenmayer describes how he became blind at the age of 13, as well as "his diligent efforts not only to pick up girls, but first to figure out which ones were attractive." In adulthood, before becoming a professional mountaineer, Weihenmayer worked as a middle school teacher and wrestling coach. Today he leads climbing expeditions with blind teenagers who live in Tibet. By the way, Erik wears two prosthetic eyes that he can pop out at will.

To read more about Erik Weihenmayer, see www.touchthetop.com/index.htm and www.climbingblind.org/Team/erik_weihenmayer.icm

emotions, we become bland and distanced from other people. You could compare this to being robot-like. We can all imagine the robots we've seen on television: they act without feeling, without caring, because they are machines. You probably know people like this, and you may have found that they can be difficult people to be around.

elf-Soothing Techniques

It's important to know that high-intensity emotions are normal during the pre-teen and teen years. Strong feelings, like anger and frustration, can be so intense that they can make you feel like you have to do something to relieve them. When you feel this way, there are things you can do to help yourself calm down and think clearly. Although it may sound simple, sometimes the best thing to do is nothing. When you're ready to explode with anger and you want to say something really mean to someone, in that moment try to find a quiet place where you stop and think about why you feel the way you do. Breathe deeply and count to ten. The courage to do nothing just might be the best antidote to strong feelings like anger and agitation.

Here are other self-soothing skills that kids have told us help them:

- Shoot hoops in the backyard or do some other physical activity
- Talk to a friend or trusted adult about how you feel
- Write about your feelings
- Listen or play music
- Decorate or tidy your room
- Draw, paint, sculpt, or do other creative activities

- Curl up under the covers with a soft pillow and watch a movie
- Take a nap

Come up with your own list of self-soothers. Regardless of what you choose to do, it's important that you learn how to handle strong feelings in a healthy way. Here are some other ideas to help you process your feelings:

- Take ten seconds to calm down
- Weigh the pros and cons of your actions
- Learn from failures
- Be flexible
- Take measured risks
- Boldly claim your dreams

Managing Anger

Anger, unlike sadness, is energizing. That is one reason why it is such a difficult emotion to control because it feeds on itself. The good news is that we can learn to be angry and yet not destructive. When we recognize that we are angry, it is best to reframe the situation. We should try to put our anger in perspective by asking ourselves questions like, "Why am I angry? Will my anger result in anything positive? What can I do to help solve the frustration I'm feeling?" These are important questions to ask because they can help you understand why you are angry and what to do about it. Yet they may also have negative effects. Be careful when you respond to your own questions so that the answers don't infuriate you more.

exercise 3.1

MANAGING EMOTIONS

Write down a time when you got really angry. Think about what caused your anger to either escalate or decline. Were you angry because you were mad at a person or at a situation?

_____

_____

_____

_____

_____

_____

_____

_____

_____

_____

_____

_____

_____

_____

_____

_____

_____

_____

_____

_____

_____

_____

_____

_____

_____

There's a proverb that says, "Better a patient man than a warrior, a man who controls his temper than one who takes a city." Anger can be the most destructive emotion because there is a certain satisfaction in being angry. It feels good to release these negative feelings because our brains tell us that it is okay. However, there is a right way to manage anger and a wrong way. The hard part is finding an *appropriate* way to express anger without harm.

We usually become angry when we are threatened in some way. Most of the time anger is not a result of a physical threat, but the result of a threat to our self-esteem or dignity. Often when we are angry it's a sign that someone has hurt our feelings. We may not recognize this at first. All we know is that we're mad at this person and we may want to get even. We can be angered when we are embarrassed or treated rudely. When we are angered, our brains are programmed to trigger what psychologists call a "fight or flight" response. That is, we are ready to fight or run for safety.

When we are angry we are much more susceptible to having other things anger us. It can be a domino effect. For example, you walk in the door after soccer practice and the first thing your mom says is that you can't play video games for a week because you didn't get a homework assignment completed on time for school. You're feeling mad about it and start walking to your room. A few seconds later, your little brother runs smack into you in the hallway because he's not watching where he's going. Even though it's an accident, this triggers your anger to erupt like a volcano. Before you know it, you push him down and yell at him for being so clumsy.

exercise 3.2

MANAGING EMOTIONS

What do you do when you become angry? Do you have ways to soothe yourself? If you do, what are they?

_____

_____

_____

_____

_____

_____

_____

_____

_____

_____

_____

_____

_____

_____

_____

_____

_____

_____

_____

_____

_____

_____

_____

_____

_____

You can control this anger in various ways, many of which you may have already read about in this chapter. Taking a walk is an excellent way to "cool off." Walking helps separate you from what is making you upset. Other ways to soothe your anger are to count to ten and breathe deeply. Exercise is also a way to release angry feelings. The release of the chemicals that takes place in our brains when we exercise overrides the chemicals in our brain that have caused us to be angry.

Who's in Control?

If you've ever tried to train your dog to sit or do some other trick, you know it's harder than it looks. Just because you have a treat in hand and you repeat the command doesn't mean Rover catches on quickly. Training takes time.

Our emotions can be like this. We may know how we're supposed to act under pressure, but staying as cool as a cucumber isn't always so simple. Certain things happen that push all our buttons and before we know it we're in a full-blown meltdown. Thankfully, there are strategies that can help:

First, we have to see ourselves as the master of our emotions. Picture yourself in a tense situation and mentally rehearse how you would like to respond. For instance, you're in the mall and the sales clerk accuses you of stealing an item off the shelf. What would be a smart way to react?

Second, if you're having trouble with managing a strong emotion like anger or discouragement, ask a friend for help. Sometimes just talking about it can be all the support you need. You can also ask your friend to hold you accountable. That's a big word that simply means your friend will check with you on how you're doing. She could simply say, "How's it going with the anger thing?" or "Have you accomplished your goal for this month?"

If you're really struggling, you may want to seek help from a counselor or other adult. The goal is to control your emotions before they control you. (See Chapter 7 for more suggestions on seeking help.)

We are starting to see how Dr. Goleman's five parts of emotional intelligence (first mentioned in Chapter 1) build on each other. Two down and three to go!

1. Self-awareness   ✓
2. Managing strong emotions   ✓
3. Self-motivation
4. Empathy
5. Managing relationships

We have learned, first, that we can be aware of our emotions, which can help us learn how to manage them. When we have the ability to manage our emotions, we are able to pay more attention to the world around us, be more creative, and stay positively motivated.

show what you know

1. *What does it mean to have "self-control"?*

_____

_____

_____

_____

_____

_____

_____

2. *Who is Erik Weihenmayer?*

_____

_____

_____

_____

_____

_____

3. *What are self-soothing skills that you can add to your life?*

_____

_____

_____

_____

_____

_____

_____

keeping your journal

In what areas of your life do you need to practice self-control?
What specific steps can you take to help gain control of that
area?

_____

_____

_____

_____

_____

_____

_____

_____

_____

_____

_____

_____

_____

_____

_____

_____

_____

_____

_____

_____

_____

_____

self-motivation

D riving at Success

Victoria's childhood was a mixed blessing. Her parents, who are high achievers, modeled a strong work ethic and a passion for life. Her mother and father pursued many interests related to their careers and hobbies. In addition to being a teacher (teacher of the year award for the district and state in her division many times), her mother also was an artist. Later, she decided that art was not enough for her and she opened her own gallery where she was also the main curator. Her father held the demanding job of real estate agent/mortgage broker.

Victoria attended a prestigious private school at a young age and, being the only child, her parents were able to buy her many luxuries, such as TVs, trips to Europe, cars, and many other things. While Victoria received everything money can buy, there was one thing she lacked: time with the ones she loved.

Victoria explains, "My parents were so busy that they didn't have time to spend with me. I saw very little of them while I was growing up, and when I did see them it was more of me being there, yet not spending time with them." And like many kids today, Victoria was pushed to be involved in many activities. "I was so overscheduled that I often felt overwhelmed and exhausted," explains Victoria. "I was involved in so many sports as a kid that today I hate participating in sports."

But Victoria also credits her parents with passing along to her their rich perspective on life. "They believed in me and allowed me to pursue my interests and gave me a sense that I could do and be anything I wanted. That's one reason I'm such

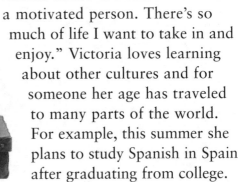

a motivated person. There's so much of life I want to take in and enjoy." Victoria loves learning about other cultures and for someone her age has traveled to many parts of the world. For example, this summer she plans to study Spanish in Spain after graduating from college.

Defining Motivation

As this story about Victoria illustrates, another important part of emotional intelligence is having the ability to be self-motivated. As you become older, self-motivation becomes a very important factor in determining the degree of success you'll have. You won't always have your parents or guardians reminding you to do stuff. It will be up to you to make things happen.

Life can get boring and monotonous. Every day can seem the same. You see the same teachers in the same classes trying to prepare you for the same tests. You eat lunch with the same friends and talk about many of the same things. The routine nature of life can cause us to become apathetic about school and other activities. That's where *self-motivation* can come in to save the day.

Self-motivation is one of the most important things to have in life. We are all faced with problems, circumstances, and situations that are not expected. When we lack the ability to motivate ourselves, we essentially lack the ability to **adapt** to a change. Let's not forget that the ability to adapt is one of the attributes that has made human existence possible!

When we adapt, we are maintaining motivation—motivation to live, motivation to succeed, and motivation to triumph over adversity. Motivation is also about **courage.** Courage is not only the ability to face danger; it is the ability to do what needs to be done to succeed, in school, at home, and in your life. Your motivation will come from your courage to make the right choice.

M anaging Anxiety

One emotion that can drain motivation is *anxiety.* The dictionary defines anxiety as "a disturbance of mind regarding some uncertain event; worry." Anxiety can be helpful or hurtful depending on how you handle it. On the one hand, some students get so overwhelmed by anxiety that they can barely function during a test. Their feelings actually make sense given the construction of the brain. The part of your brain that causes anxiety cuts off the part of your brain where memories are stored. On the other hand, some students do exceedingly well when under pressure. Several theories can tell us why this is, but none of them are as important as maintaining a positive attitude through self-awareness and emotional management.

SANDY RIVERA

Self-Motivation, Optimism, Adaptability

Sandy grew up in a troubled household, the third child of six siblings. Her father drank heavily and routinely took out his bad mood on those he should have loved and protected most, his family. Sandy recalls her father hitting her mother, "My brother, sister, and I would try to stop him, but then he would turn to hitting us. He would scream mean, nasty stuff at us."

Eventually, Sandy's older sister ran away from home at the age of sixteen because she could no longer handle the abuse. A year later, her older brother left as well. To avoid being at home when her father was there, Sandy began staying out late and hanging out with people who reinforced her increasingly negative attitude about life. Sandy's heart staggered under the weight of her loneliness.

In junior high, Sandy became a member of the I Have a Dream Foundation, an organization that provides ongoing academic support for disadvantaged children. The program coordinator for the organization could see that Sandy needed a fresh start, so he helped Sandy transfer into a new middle school, away from the corroding influences that threatened to suffocate her potential.

At first, Sandy's grades and outlook did improve, but once she started high school she fell back into a self-destructive cycle of negative thinking and quiet desperation. The rage she felt toward her father had been building inside her, and the only thing that seemed to numb the pain were parties and drugs. She became mentally trapped in a downward spiral of hopelessness. Her inner light was going out.

Once again, the Foundation's coordinator intervened. He described a school in the mountains of Colorado that could give Sandy the opportunity to escape the hurt that plagued her. Perhaps the majesty of soaring peaks and the love of people who cared about hurting kids could help Sandy's spirit heal. Sandy agreed to give it a try.

When she arrived, Sandy, along with a group of other new students, was taken on an exhausting, 23-day excursion into the wilderness, camping and hiking while carrying an 80-pound backpack. Sandy had never camped before. There were difficult days, and at times she felt like quitting, but she knew she had nowhere to go but up. So with an enormous display of pure willpower, Sandy pressed on.

With each passing day, Sandy's confidence grew, and she began to feel at peace with her stormy past. The stony tomb that had once imprisoned Sandy's heart began to crumble under newfound hope. By remaining open to new experiences, and relying on the advice of a trusted friend from the Foundation, Sandy was able to adapt to a different life from the one she grew up in, one where broken hearts are repaired and dreams are rescued.

Looking back, Sandy describes herself as being a "pointy, jagged stone that no one would want to hold." Then she discovered an opportunity to make a change, and in spite of her doubts about herself and her future, she took a chance. Sandy now describes herself as, "the smooth stone that you want to hold in your hand." She explains that she got that way just as a river rock becomes smooth, rolling and tumbling through experiences that have helped shape her into the person that she is today.

Adapted from *Trail Mix* by Danielle Corriveau; Corvo Communications, 2001.

exercise 4.1

SELF-MOTIVATION

Describe someone you know who has pressed on and achieved success despite many hardships and obstacles. This person might be a role model for you. What do you think motivated that person to keep going?

_____

_____

_____

_____

_____

_____

_____

_____

_____

_____

_____

_____

_____

_____

_____

_____

_____

_____

_____

_____

_____

_____

_____

It has been tested and verified that students who maintain a positive attitude about their schoolwork will receive better grades and have more fun learning. If we keep a positive and optimistic outlook on the challenges ahead of us, we can actually regulate our emotions and stay focused on success. As we discussed in Chapter Three, when we can control how we feel by understanding our emotions, we have true control over our futures.

ustaining Hope

Motivation is also about **hope.** When we think of people who have survived horrible situations, it was often their internal motivation that kept them from giving up. When we have a positive "can do" attitude about our ability to solve problems, then we have a better chance of improving the outcome than when we are pessimistic. For example, if you received a D on your first test of the semester, you may develop a negative mindset about being able to finish the semester with an A or a B. If you maintain the *hope* that you can figure out a way to make the class a success, your chances are better than if you give up on being able to make a decent grade. Students who maintain a positive and hopeful attitude after a disappointment will do better than students who don't.

mpulse Control

Making smart life choices has much to do with your ability to control impulses. *Impulse control* takes discipline. One type of discipline is called "delayed gratification." This means working hard now to get something better in the future. For instance, in a study by Daniel Goleman, several children were tested on their ability to delay gratification by controlling their impulses. Each child was given one marshmallow and promised another if they resisted eating it for 15 to 20 minutes. Or, if they didn't want to wait, they could ring a bell to let the experimenters know that they wanted to eat the marshmallow. If they decided to eat the marshmallow, then they would receive no more.

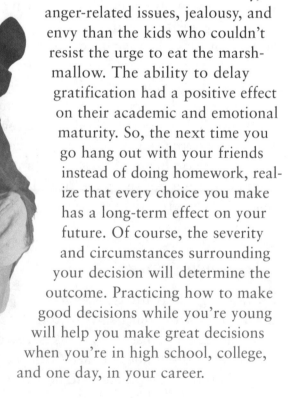

Interestingly, these same students were surveyed two years later, and it was found that the students who delayed gratification during that experiment also got better grades and suffered from fewer emotional distresses like test anxiety, anger-related issues, jealousy, and envy than the kids who couldn't resist the urge to eat the marshmallow. The ability to delay gratification had a positive effect on their academic and emotional maturity. So, the next time you go hang out with your friends instead of doing homework, realize that every choice you make has a long-term effect on your future. Of course, the severity and circumstances surrounding your decision will determine the outcome. Practicing how to make good decisions while you're young will help you make great decisions when you're in high school, college, and one day, in your career.

exercise 4.2

SELF-MOTIVATION

Think about a time when you needed to motivate yourself and how your motivation helped you succeed. Write out the situation below.

_____

_____

_____

_____

_____

_____

_____

_____

_____

_____

_____

Now think of a time when you were unable to motivate yourself. What happened as a result of your lack of motivation?

_____

_____

_____

_____

_____

_____

_____

_____

_____

_____

_____

Just like the kids in the marshmallow experiment, when you've learned to put off what will satisfy an emotional craving you are more successful in life. Whether we are putting off watching TV until we finish our homework or deciding if we should skip school to go skiing, it is important to realize that your life is made up of these types of choices. Not everything will be fun, but if you know deep down that having the discipline to stay on task will help you in the long run, you're already halfway to being a healthy, emotionally intelligent person.

Motivation comes from the ability to delay gratification and to control impulses. When we control our impulses, we shut out any distractions that may keep us from completing the task at hand. The ability to focus on goal accomplishment and being able to delay gratification are good ways to measure your level of emotional intelligence. When you are then capable of finishing what you have started, moving on to the next goal in your life will be less challenging.

Flow

Have you ever played a sport where everything you did was perfect? Have you ever painted a picture that seemed to paint itself? Maybe you've written an essay that seemed easy because the words just poured onto the paper. These kinds of effortless experiences, when we sense we are in a mental zone of concentration, can be referred to as "flow." Flow is ultimate focus. For example, a surgeon who had just finished a long and difficult operation was surprised to find a pile of rubble next to his feet. When he asked the nurse what had happened, she explained that the ceiling had caved in above him. He had been in such a focused state that he had not noticed.

We are constantly regulating our mood between boredom and feelings of anxiety. We need a little anxiety to be productive because if there were no sense of urgency or need to get something done, we wouldn't do what needs to be done. At the same time if we were totally anxiety ridden our minds could not operate effectively. Flow comes when we find the perfect spot between boredom and anxiety. When we are relaxed, determined, and motivated we can operate at a very high level. Furthermore, when we are *flowing* the activity is not tiresome; it is invigorating.

Here are a few suggestions to help you stay motivated:

- Keep your goals in mind
- Write and remember how you feel when you accomplish a goal
- Try to find at least one thing you like about your classes and everyday activities

Virtual Reality

If you've ever tried on a pair of virtual reality goggles, you know how it simulates realistic 3-D images. You see different scenes and feel as if you're a part of the action. It's a similar kind of vision that can help you stay motivated. People who have a vision, a picture of what they want to achieve, usually control their destiny and lifestyle. For people without a vision, their destiny and lifestyle are often controlled by others.

One of the best ways to get motivated is to discover your natural talent. Knowing what you're really good at can motivate you to keep trying. Super achievers have a goal, a mental picture of what they want to achieve.

show what you know

DEMONSTRATE YOUR UNDERSTANDING

1. *What is self-motivation? Define it.*

_____

_____

_____

_____

_____

_____

_____

2. *Who is Sandy Rivera?*

_____

_____

_____

_____

_____

_____

_____

3. *Why do you think some people are more motivated than others?*

_____

_____

_____

_____

_____

_____

_____

keeping your journal

In what areas of life have you demonstrated motivation? In what areas have you procrastinated or not been motivated? What do you think could help you become more self-motivated?

_____

_____

_____

_____

_____

_____

_____

_____

_____

_____

_____

_____

_____

_____

_____

_____

_____

_____

_____

_____

_____

_____

_____

CHAPTER FIVE

developing social skills

Yvette was just 8 years old when the genocide started in her native country of Rwanda, in Africa, in April of 1994. (*Genocide* means the systematic killing of racial and national groups.) More than 250 members of her extended family were killed in one of the worst massacres in recorded history. She and her older nephew, who was 12 years old at the time, hid in the swamps of the jungle. There they ate bugs and leaves to stay alive. Finally, after six weeks of misery, they were rescued.

Today, Yvette is a high school graduate living in the United States. She plans to go to college and major in art because drawing and painting have become therapeutic for her. The hardest part has been the insensitivity of some people over what she's been through. "If they knew how horrible I feel inside at times; if they knew about the awful nightmares I have, I think they would be nicer to me," she explains.

Yvette's aunt, who was living in the United States at the time of the genocide, wrote a moving article about her father for her college newspaper. Part of it reads: "I learned from Papa that reaching out to others is an important moral value. . . . I would like to pass on what you gave me so the world can be a better place, because in the end, we are all one."

Making Global Connections

This is one reason why social studies is an important part of your education; it helps you to understand that we live in a global society and to appreciate other cultures different from your own. Although most of us may never meet someone who has suffered to the extent that Yvette and her aunt have, we can all become aware of the struggles people are facing in other parts of the world, and this knowledge can motivate us to make a difference.

The key to becoming connected globally is to start small, right where you are. Rake leaves at no charge for the lady next door, volunteer at a retirement home, become a pen pal with someone who lives in another country, or help younger children at youth camps. Even learning more about events like the Summer and Winter Olympics can give you a sense of our global connectedness. The point is to do something with what you know.

Humans are *social* beings. We live together, work together, and have fun together. For most of us, we do this almost every day. You can also think of *social skills* as the ability to cooperate and get along with others. Although it is important to be polite, we must also think about other aspects that influence our relationships.

L istening

First, we must learn to listen. When we listen to others, this shows we value their thoughts and ideas. Listening is a great way to understand where other people are coming from. It is also easy to tell when someone is not listening to what we have to say. We all have experienced this and probably have been guilty of not listening ourselves. Listening is a skill, and like any skill it takes practice. While you are in a conversation, you can learn to pay attention and think of questions to ask the person to follow up on what's been said. This is called *active listening* and it's an important part of carrying on a conversation. This shows the other person that you *care* about what they are saying. If you pay close attention to their words, the speaker will feel connected to you, as the listener. After all, when you speak you want the person hearing your message to listen to you. Active listening is a way of showing respect.

Here are a few more things to consider when you talk to other people:

- Learn to listen first and ask questions second.
- Look people in the eye and be confident when you speak.
- Be honest; people will be able to tell when you aren't.
- Show people you understand, by nodding your head or saying "I see." When you don't understand something, ask them what they mean.

Seeing Emotions in Others

When we understand the feelings and emotions of others, we are socially aware. We should always try to interact with confidence and respect. Daniel Goleman, the Yale psychologist who coined the term *emotional intelligence* and whom we mentioned in Chapter One, explains that when people don't control their impulses they may have difficulties socially. To become emotionally intelligent, we must show self-control so that we don't hurt ourselves or those around us.

If you've ever volunteered at a hospital, you know that lots of people experience many different emotions there. That's because being injured or sick physically also affects people emotionally, yet there may also be people in the hospital who are extremely happy, such as mothers experiencing the joy of having a new baby.

Even if you haven't observed people in a hospital setting, you can imagine nurses moving around with urgency, parents holding their new babies, doctors being concerned for the welfare of a sick patient, or family members grieving over the loss of a loved one. Although a hospital is an extreme example of a place where people experience a variety of emotions, thinking about how people might feel in different situations can help us become more socially aware.

Emotions are very strong feelings that can have much control over our day-to-day activities, as well as our outlook on life. If we always let feelings dominate our existence we may find our lives to be somewhat chaotic. The trick isn't to ignore how we feel but rather to use our feelings to sense how others may be feeling.

Here are some activities that promote social awareness:

- Working as a volunteer
- Observing and describing the feelings of others in your journal
- Developing a compassionate heart by noticing the needs of those around you
- Gaining perspective by comparing your life to the lives of others

mpathy
Defining Empathy

Empathy is the ability to understand what others are feeling. It's being able to put yourself in someone else's shoes and imagine how you would feel if you were in their place. When you can accurately perceive how someone else feels, then you can gauge what is the most appropriate response. For example, your reaction to someone who has just lost a loved one will be very different from the reaction you would give to someone who has just won a game. These examples point out that when you recognize how others feel, you'll have a better chance to communicate with them effectively.

We all, at one time or another, have heard about something sad, disappointing, or otherwise discouraging that happened to someone else. You may even have heard about something first hand, from the person to whom it actually happened. Do you remember what you were thinking as the person told you the story? How did you feel? Were you glad it hadn't happened to you? The feelings we have about someone else's

KIM MEEDER

Co-founder of "The Ranch of Rescued Dreams"

K im Meeder will never forget the horrible day when a relative came to school to pick her up, and her older sister, and made the long drive to her grandparents' home. She knew something terrible had happened but didn't know what.

When they arrived at the house, a crowd of people stood around grieving. Someone reached for 9-year-old Kim and proceeded to explain the inconceivable: Kim's father had murdered her mother and then killed himself. Her parents had been going through a divorce, and her father couldn't accept that he was losing his family.

Kim ran out the back door, her eyes blinded with tears. "I was trying desperately to run from the incomprehensible. Everything I knew to be safe and right were gone," she later said.

A short time later, Kim and her sister went to live with their grandmother, where they were introduced to horses. Riding quickly became a healing refuge for Kim, and she credits her first little pony with saving her life from the emotional shock of her parents' violent deaths.

This saving grace was a portent of what was to come years later, when Kim and her husband Troy made the decision to transform a former rock quarry into a small ranch. In 1996, Crystal Peaks Youth Ranch, also known as the "Ranch of Rescued Dreams," opened in central Oregon. This unique organization rescues abused and neglected horses and pairs them with disadvantaged children. The ranch's mission is to "pair one child with one horse, guided by one leader, 100 percent of the time." Although the ranch activities are designed for youth at risk, all children of all ages are welcome, free of charge. In 2004 Kim Meeder's commitment was nationally recognized with the Jefferson Award for Public Service.

Adapted from *Hope Rising: Stories from the Ranch of Rescued Dreams*. Sisters, OR: Multnomah Publishers, 2003.

situation can tell a great deal about how we think about life, our future, and what we desire from our lives.

As stated above, the ability to identify and feel what another person is feeling is called *empathy.* Of course, we can never feel *exactly* what others are feeling, but through self-awareness we are able to better understand the feelings of others. From the start of this book, we have been trying to discover who we are, why we do what we do, why we feel the way we do, and how this knowledge of personal discovery will help motivate us to live a productive and happy life. In the same way that we use emotional intelligence to help ourselves, we can also use these tools to understand and help other people.

Communicating Empathy

Why is it important to know how and why people feel the way they do? Imagine going to school and having no idea of how anyone around you is feeling. Could you still talk about the things you usually talk about? Would your friends still be your friends if you couldn't so much as read their facial expressions, tone of voice, body movements, or gestures? These are all means of communication, and when we don't communicate effectively there may be a misunderstanding. Have you ever been misunderstood? If you have, then you probably felt frustrated and probably angry or disappointed. Lack of emotional intelligence can hurt and even destroy relationships.

exercise 5.1

EMPATHY

Remember a time when you shared in someone else's pain. How were you able to help this person? How did their hurt affect you?

_____

_____

_____

_____

_____

_____

_____

_____

_____

_____

Now remember a time when someone else shared your pain. What did they do that showed they understood how you were feeling and that they cared?

_____

_____

_____

_____

_____

_____

_____

_____

_____

_____

When you listen to someone else, strive not only to hear the words but also to hear what the person is feeling. By hearing their feelings on a certain subject, you will be more in tune with the *true* situation. How many times have we listened to someone's story, even that of a close friend, and said, "Oh that's too bad," and given the issue little thought. Our ability to comprehend the feelings of the people around us is our degree of empathy.

Empathy is a skill that can be improved through self-awareness and a personal desire to show compassion. When you try to understand what a person is saying, your mind will automatically generate questions to ask. By asking these questions, you are not only discovering why the person feels the way he or she does, you are also showing the person that you care about what they are experiencing. That person, in turn, will feel recognized and important.

Bullies Beware!

Of all the social problems students face, bullying is by far one of the worst. Many bullies share some common characteristics. They like to dominate others and are generally self-centered. They also often have poor social skills and social judgment.

To help insulate yourself against bullying, don't go it alone. Surround yourself with true friends and get involved in extracurricular activities. Bullies tend to target students who they think don't fit in or who are shy. Here are some other things you can do to combat physical and verbal bullying, according to the web site Kids Health.org. They're also good tips to share with a friend as a way to show your support:

MEAN GIRLS AIN'T NOTHIN' NEW

by Jennifer Amanda Keller

My bully wasn't the older mean boy who smelled bad and pushed me around on the playground. My bully didn't look like a wanna-be gangsta.

My bullies were two pretty girls in the latest fashions who made the grades and came from nice families.

No, they didn't beat me up after school. No, they didn't steal my lunch money. From third grade all the way through high school, one of their extracurricular activities was ridiculing me and keeping me just close enough in their social circle that they could stiff-arm me and know that it would hurt. Why they were bullies, I'll never know.

They were just being *girls,* you could say. However, not all girls growing up consistently find avenues to put other kids down and make it hurt. It was like they had a sixth sense to find any kid's weakest point: they'd make fun of the fat kid for eating two ice cream sandwiches at lunch or taunt the girl from the trailer park because she wore the same jacket every day. I was the target for some of their best bullying: the shy girl who really needed some friends. I was originally drawn to them because everyone knew them and they were the smart, outgoing girls. We were in the same class, I liked the clothes they wore (even though my folks couldn't afford clothes like that), and we even had afterschool dance classes together. I thought I had found true friends.

Then the teasing started. I was one of the few kids in the third grade with glasses. Then add some braces and a bad perm to that in fourth grade. Then add the fact that I was one of the tallest girls in my class—much taller than all of the boys. My bullies were short and cute and didn't have glasses or braces. I became a "four-eyed railroad track", a "bean-pole," and then in eighth grade (my personal favorite put-down), "You're so flat you make the walls jealous!" They'd pretend to be interested in which boy I liked, only to embarrass me in front of him.

They also knew how to manipulate people. One afternoon at recess they made fun of one of my good friends: she definitely wasn't in the "cool" crowd, didn't have the clothes or the latest Swatch Watch. After my friend ran off crying, they gave me an ultimatum: "If you talk to her, you're out! It's her or us!" It was a difficult choice at the time: I wanted them to accept me. . . . I wanted to be "in." But I didn't like how they treated other people. After a couple of minutes, I ran after my Swatch Watch–less friend, and needless to say things went downhill from there.

The worst experience I had with them was as a freshman in high school. My locker was near one of the girl's lockers, and one day between classes they enlisted their senior jock boyfriends to trap me in the hallway. They all gathered around as the boyfriends dropped F-bombs, mocked me, and called me names. The girls stood and laughed as they watched me squirm in embarrassment and shock. One of my friends finally came over to break it up. I was devastated!

I spent more than a couple of years being angry at my bullies and waiting for the day they became fat and ugly. Then in the summer after our sophomore year, one of our mutual friends was killed in a car accident. We cried together and talked about our friend and wished the accident hadn't happened. We never became best friends, but I think going through our friend's death helped us realize that life is a gift and there's no time for bullying or bitterness.

Reprinted by permission of the author.

- **Ignore the bully and walk away.** It's definitely not a coward's response— sometimes it can be harder than losing your temper. Bullies thrive on the reaction they get, and if you walk away, or ignore hurtful emails or instant messages, you're telling the bully that you just don't care. Sooner or later the bully will probably get bored with trying to bother you.

- **Disarm the bully.** If you're in a situation where you have to deal with a bully and can't walk away with poise, use humor—it can throw the bully off guard.

- **Avoid getting physical.** However you choose to deal with a bully, most experts say you should avoid using physical force (like kicking, hitting, or pushing). Not only are you showing your anger, which is what the bully wants, but you can never be sure what the bully will do in response.

- **Talk about it.** It may help to talk to a guidance counselor, teacher, or friend—anyone who can give you the support you need. Talking can be a good outlet for the fears and frustrations that can build when you're being bullied.

Another way to combat bullying is to join your school's anti-violence program. If there's one, talk with your principal about your ideas. By taking a stand against bullying you'll encourage other students to do the same.

show what you know

1. What are social skills? Define them.

_____

_____

_____

_____

_____

_____

_____

2. Who is Kim Meeder?

_____

_____

_____

_____

_____

_____

_____

3. How does a person demonstrate empathy?

_____

_____

_____

_____

_____

_____

_____

keeping your journal

GET IN TOUCH WITH HOW YOU FEEL

When was the last time you were in an uncomfortable social situation? What happened and how did you handle it? How could you have handled it better?

_____

_____

_____

_____

_____

_____

_____

_____

_____

_____

_____

_____

_____

_____

_____

_____

_____

_____

_____

_____

_____

_____

_____

_____

_____

CHAPTER SIX

stress

Katrina often feels that there are too many pressures and demands on her. Lately, she's been losing sleep worrying about tests and schoolwork. She often eats on the run and doesn't exercise regularly because "life's too busy." Katrina is not alone. Everyone experiences stress at times—adults, teens, and even kids. But there are things you can do to minimize stress and manage the stress that's unavoidable.

What Is Stress?

Stress is a feeling that's created when we react to particular events. It's the body's way of rising to a challenge and preparing to meet a tough situation with focus, strength, stamina, and heightened alertness. The events that provoke stress are called *stressors,* and they cover a whole range of situations—everything from outright physical danger to making a class presentation to going through a breakup with a boyfriend or girlfriend.

Not all stress is bad. If we didn't ever feel a sense of urgency, we might not accomplish very much in life. But pressures that are too intense or last too long, or troubles that are shouldered alone, can cause people to feel stress overload. Here are some of the things that can overwhelm the body's ability to cope if they continue for a long time:

- Being bullied or exposed to violence or injury
- Relationship stress, family conflicts, or the heavy emotions that can accompany a broken heart or the death of a loved one
- Ongoing problems with schoolwork related to a learning disability or other problems, such as ADHD (once the problem is recognized and the person is given the right learning support, the stress usually disappears)
- Crammed schedules, not having enough time to rest and relax, and always being on the go

Some stressful situations can be extreme and may require special attention and professional care. Posttraumatic stress disorder is a very strong stress reaction that can develop in people who have lived through an extremely traumatic event, such as a serious car accident, a natural disaster like an earthquake, or an assault like rape.

Some people have anxiety problems that can cause them to overreact to stress, making even small difficulties seem like crises. If a person frequently feels tense, upset, worried, or stressed, it may be a sign of anxiety. Anxiety problems usually need attention, and many people turn to professional counselors for help in overcoming them. According to the U.S. Department of Health and Human Services, one in ten kids suffer from an anxiety disorder.

S igns of Stress Overload

"Everyone experiences stress a little differently," explains licensed clinical social worker Lisa Schab, who also writes about teen issues for *Chicago Parent,* a monthly news-magazine. "Some people become angry and act out their stress or take it out on others. Some people internalize it and develop eating disorders or substance abuse problems. And some people who have a chronic illness may find that the symptoms of their illness flare up under an overload of stress."

According to the National Institute of Mental Health, people who are experiencing stress overload may notice some of the following signs:

- Anxiety or panic attacks
- A feeling of being constantly pressured, hassled, and hurried
- Irritability and moodiness
- Physical symptoms, such as stomach problems, headaches, or even chest pain
- Allergic reactions, such as eczema or asthma
- Problems sleeping
- Drinking too much, smoking, overeating, or doing drugs
- Sadness or depression

Some behavioral issues can mask emotional distress or unhappiness and discontent in a person's life. These behaviors may include the following:

- Bullying
- Busyness (over-scheduling to mask feeling of inadequacy or hurt)
- Cutting (a form of self-injury)
- Eating disorders
- Joining gangs
- Becoming sexually active before you're ready
- Passivity and apathy (the opposite of being too busy)
- Substance abuse and other addictions

Schab says that she sees two types of stress repeatedly in her counseling work with teens: cutting and achievement anxiety.

Cutting

Injuring yourself on purpose by making scratches or cuts on your body with a sharp object—enough to break the skin and make it bleed—is called "cutting." The urge to cut might be triggered by strong feelings the person can't express—such as anger, hurt, shame, frustration, or depression. People who cut sometimes say they feel they don't fit in or that no one understands them. A person might cut because of losing someone close or to escape a sense of emptiness. Schab says, "Cutting might seem like the only way to find relief, or the only way to express personal pain over relationships or rejection. Yet even people who cut agree that cutting isn't a good way to get that relief. For one thing, the relief doesn't last—the troubles that triggered the cutting remain, they're just masked over." This is the issue behind many antisocial or self-destructive behaviors: the behaviors mask what's behind the emotional distress.

BETHANY HAMILTON

"Most Courageous Teen"

On Halloween morning of 2003, 13-year-old Bethany Hamilton was attacked by a tiger shark while surfing in Hawaii. The 15-foot-long beast bit off her arm just below the shoulder and also chomped a huge chunk from her surfboard. Before the attack, Bethany was the state's top-ranked female amateur surfer. Many wondered if she'd ever get back in the water.

Amazingly, just months after the attack, Bethany is surfing competitively again, and she aims to be among the world's best surfers. In 2004, she won the Teen Choice Award for "Most Courageous Teen," and *YM* magazine dubbed her "The Bravest Girl in America." She's also appeared on television, on such such shows as *The Oprah Winfrey Show, 20/20,* and *Good Morning America.*

Bethany says that all the attention has brought about its share of stresses, and she's learning to cope. In her new book *Soul Surfer* she explains:

> I often dream that I have both my arms again, and I wake up expecting the whole shark business to be a nightmare. But it's not . . . I am still learning how to cope every day. I'm not talking about learning how to button my top with one hand. I'm talking about coping with being a celebrity, something I never imagined that I would have to deal with at the age of fourteen. . . . All the attention and activity gets in the way of my being able to do things I want to do . . . like hanging with my friends or surfing. I even got way behind in my schoolwork and had to cram and work really hard to catch up.

Through it all, Bethany's spiritual centeredness and family support remain strong: "I want to use what happened to me as an opportunity to tell people that God is worthy of our trust, and to show them that you can go on and do wonderful things in spite of terrible events that happen." Bethany is certainly living proof of that.

Adapted from Bethany Hamilton's web site, www.bethanyhamilton.com

Achievement Anxiety

According to Schab, high expectations about getting into college have raised the stress levels of young teens dramatically. "Decent grades and a written essay no longer are enough," Schab says. "Increasing achievement pressure on kids can actually hinder their ability to get ahead. A teen who gets into Harvard but picks up an anxiety disorder along the way isn't headed for success. Kids and their parents need to realize the importance of emotional health for success in life," she declares.

Healthy Ways to Cope with Stress

Many good, healthy ways exist for coping with difficulties, such as talking with parents, other adults, or friends; putting problems in perspective; and taking time for activities you enjoy like journaling, listening to your favorite music, meditating, practicing yoga, and any other healthy, uplifting activity. The following are other practical suggestions from KidsHealth.org for coping with stress:*

● **Take a stand against over-scheduling.** If you're feeling stretched, consider dropping an activity or two, opting for just the ones that are most important to you.

● **Be realistic.** Don't try to be perfect—no one is. And expecting others to be perfect can add to your stress level, too (not to mention put a lot of pressure on them!). If you need help on something, like schoolwork, ask for it.

This information in this list was provided by KidsHealth, one of the largest resources online for medically reviewed health information written for parents, kids, and teens. For more articles like this one, visit www.KidsHealth.org or www.TeensHealth.org. ©1995–2005. The Nemours Foundation.

- **Get a good night's sleep.** Getting enough sleep helps keep your body and mind in top shape, making you better equipped to deal with any negative stressors. Because the biological "sleep clock" shifts during adolescence, many teens prefer staying up a little later at night and sleeping a little later in the morning. But if you stay up late and still need to get up early for school, you may not get all the hours of sleep you need.

- **Treat your body well.** Experts agree that getting regular exercise helps people manage stress. (Excessive or compulsive exercise can contribute to stress, though, so, as in all things, use moderation.) Eat well to help your body get the right fuel to function at its best. It's easy when you're stressed out to eat on the run or eat junk food or fast food. But under stressful conditions, the body needs its vitamins and minerals more than ever. Some people may turn to substance abuse as a way to ease tension. Although alcohol or drugs may seem to lift the stress temporarily, relying on them to cope with stress actually promotes more stress because it wears down the body's ability to bounce back.

- **Watch what you're thinking.** Your outlook, attitude, and thoughts influence the way you see things. Is your cup half full or half empty? A healthy dose of optimism can help you make the best of stressful circumstances. Even if you're out of practice, or tend to be a bit of a pessimist, everyone can learn to think more optimistically and reap the benefits.

- **Solve the little problems.** Learning to solve everyday problems can give you a sense of control. But avoiding them can leave you feeling helpless, and that just adds to stress. Develop skills to calmly look at a problem, figure out options, and take some action toward a solution. Feeling capable of solving little problems builds the inner confidence to move on to life's bigger ones— and it can serve you well in times of stress.

  • **Learn to relax.** The body's natural antidote to stress is called the relaxation response. It's your body's opposite of stress, and it creates a sense of well-being and calm. The chemical benefits of the relaxation response can be activated simply by relaxing. You can help trigger the relaxation response by learning simple breathing exercises and then using them when you're caught up in stressful situations. Ensure you stay relaxed by building time into your schedule for activities that are calming and pleasurable: reading a good book or making time for a hobby, spending time with your pet, or just taking a relaxing bath.

Building Your Resilience

Ever notice that certain people seem to adapt quickly to stressful circumstances and take things in stride? They're cool under pressure and able to handle problems as they come up. Researchers have identified the qualities that make some people seem naturally resilient even when faced with high levels of stress. If you want to build your resilience, work on developing these attitudes and behaviors:

  • Think of change as a challenging but normal part of life.
  • See setbacks and problems as temporary and solvable.
  • Believe that you will succeed if you keep working toward your goals.
  • Take action to solve problems that crop up rather than waiting until they're full-blown to do something.

- Build strong relationships and keep commitments to family and friends.
- Have a support system and ask for help.
- Participate regularly in activities for relaxation and fun.
- Let a little stress motivate you into positive action to reach your goals.

etting in Touch with Wisdom from Ancient Cultures

We can also learn valuable lessons about dealing with emotional upsets by turning to the wisdom of ancient cultures. Here are four methods that have been used in the past for reducing stress and enhancing well-being:

- Dancing
- Singing
- Story telling
- Silence

Tapping your own inner wisdom and passions by spending time alone or attending camps and youth retreats can also help you soothe anxieties and find your own internal compass for making healthy life choices.

ilencing the Inner Critic

Not all stressors come from the outside; some come from inside. Constant criticism can harm self-esteem—and it doesn't always come from others. Some teens have an "inner critic," a voice inside that seems to find fault with everything they do—and self-esteem obviously has a hard time growing when that happens. Some people have modeled their inner critic's voice after a critical parent or teacher whose acceptance was important to them. The good news is that this inner critic can be restrained; because it now belongs to you, you can be the one to decide that the inner critic will give only constructive feedback from now on.

etting Healthy Boundaries

Boundaries come in two forms: *physical boundaries* represent the space between you and another person, and *emotional boundaries* are lines you draw in terms of how you let other people treat you. For example, suppose you have a friend who constantly shares your secrets with other people. Unless you let him know how you feel, he will never know that he is crossing a boundary. If you do make your feelings known and he continues with the behavior that bothers you, however, he isn't respecting your feelings—he is overstepping that boundary. Knowing your own boundaries puts you in a better position to recognize when you're in a potentially dangerous situation.

If you're having trouble setting boundaries, you may

want to consider taking a self-defense class at your local community center or college. These programs are designed to empower you in all kinds of ways, from learning to use your intuition (inner voice) to redirecting and de-escalating the behavior of a bully.

Seeking Help

Healthy, successful people have had huge challenges to deal with, and they've learned how to get help so their issues don't become liabilities. Getting help is a sign of strength, not weakness. Many people are available and want to help you; you just need to take the first step and ask for what you need.

show what you know

1. What is stress? Define it.

_____

_____

_____

_____

_____

_____

_____

_____

2. Who is Bethany Hamilton?

_____

_____

_____

_____

_____

_____

_____

_____

3. List seven healthy ways to cope with stress.

_____

_____

_____

_____

_____

_____

_____

keeping your journal

GET IN TOUCH WITH HOW YOU FEEL

1. What are your stress triggers? When was the last time you were in a highly stressful situation? Describe what happened and how you handled it.

_____

_____

_____

_____

_____

_____

_____

_____

_____

_____

2. How would you like to handle situations like this in the future? Could these sorts of situations help you become better at managing or avoiding high levels of stress?

_____

_____

_____

_____

_____

_____

_____

_____

_____

_____

CHAPTER SEVEN

using emotional intelligence

Being a Team Player

If you've ever worked with other classmates on a school project or competed in sports or other extracurricular activities, you know the importance of teamwork. If one person on your team is a ball hog or if one classmate wants all the credit for an assignment, you know how it hurts the team as a whole. Teams are meant to work together, not against each other. Being a team player is about sharing the credit and contributing your ideas and abilities so that everyone wins.

Being a Leader

Do you ever think, "I can't wait until I grow up and I'm in charge"? Because you're young, it probably looks to you like everybody's in charge but you. Everywhere you turn, there's

81

somebody else telling you what to do. Yet the reality is you do have opportunities to lead; the key is to recognize those opportunities and then to make the most of them.

One trait you see most often in leaders is that they take initiative. This means they take the first step to make something better. You can do the same. Don't wait for someone to tell you what to do; think about what needs to be done and do it. If someone else is running things, offer your ideas and explain how you'd like to help. Then if you're given the green light, go for it. Over time you'll develop a mindset to make a difference.

Being a Positive Influence

It should be called the "embarrassment card." In soccer, if you do something really bad, the referee runs over to you, pulls a red card out of his or her pocket, and shoves it in your face. You have just been kicked out of the game. Most professional soccer teams make it their goal to avoid getting any red cards.

That's a great goal for all of us, even if we're not playing pro soccer. Even if we're playing a little one on one in the driveway or a game of Scrabble in the family room, this goal is something to aim for.

Making a good impression by staying under control goes far beyond how you act on the soccer field. It also should show up in all kinds of situations. At school when a friend says something that insults you, how do you respond? At band practice when you don't get the recognition you thought you deserved for something you did, do you threaten to quit? At home when your little brother or sister takes one of your CDs, do you get even? Day after day you will face situations where people will be noticing what you say and what you do.

Want to avoid getting a red card? Learn to know what the officials are looking for. Here are some of the violations that can earn you a red card:

- Committing an act of violence or a serious foul
- Using foul or abusive language
- Continuing to break the rules after a caution.

Being a positive influence means staying under control when things don't go your way. Someone once said, "A person wrapped up in himself makes a very small package."

Emotional Intelligence and Talking It Over

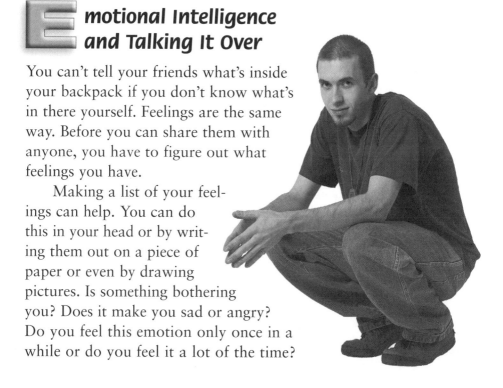

You can't tell your friends what's inside your backpack if you don't know what's in there yourself. Feelings are the same way. Before you can share them with anyone, you have to figure out what feelings you have.

Making a list of your feelings can help. You can do this in your head or by writing them out on a piece of paper or even by drawing pictures. Is something bothering you? Does it make you sad or angry? Do you feel this emotion only once in a while or do you feel it a lot of the time?

When you're trying to figure out your feelings, it might help to remember something that happened and think about how it made you feel. Then you can say, "I feel sad when my friend ignores me," or "I feel angry when my brother always wins at soccer." This can help you figure out your own feelings. It also gives the person you're talking with more information about what's bothering you.

Why Talk About Your Feelings?

The way a person feels inside is important. It can be really hard not to tell anyone that you're feeling sad, worried, or upset. Then it's just you and these bad feelings. If you keep feelings locked inside, it can even make you feel sick!

But if you talk with someone who cares for you, like your mom or dad, you will almost always start to feel better. Now you're not all alone with your problems or worries. It doesn't mean your problems and worries disappear magically, but at least someone else knows what's bothering you and can help you find solutions.

Your mom and dad want to know if you have problems because they love you and they want to know what's happening in your life. But what if a kid doesn't want to talk with his or her parents? Then find another trusted adult, like a relative or a counselor at school. Maybe this person can help you talk with your mom and dad about your problem or concern.

How to Talk About Your Feelings

Once you know who you can talk with, you'll want to pick a time and place to talk. Does it need to be private, or can you talk with your brother and sister in

HAROLD ABRAMS

Running to Win

Harold Abrams was annoyed. He had just run an early heat in the 100-yard dash, and he stunk. It was the Olympic Games of 1924 (the Olympics made famous in the movie *Chariots of Fire*), and Abrams was expected to win. He ran well enough to qualify for the finals, but he felt terrible about his race.

He was so disgusted with himself that after he finished his heat, he walked over to where his fiancée was sitting and told her, "I won't run anymore if I can't win."

To which she replied, "If you don't run, you can't win." Her response was brilliant yet simple.

Abrams listened to his fiancée and proceeded to go out on the track and win an Olympic gold in the 100-yard dash. And he set an Olympic record, too.

Adapted from *Heads Up: Sports Devotions for All-Star Kids*, by Dave Branon. Zonderkidz, 2000.

the room? If you think you'll have trouble saying what's on your mind, write it down on a piece of paper. If the person doesn't understand what you mean right away, try explaining it a different way or give an example of what's concerning you. Is there something you think could be done to make things better? If so, say it.

Some kids—just like some adults—are more private than others. That means some people will feel more shy about sharing their feelings. You don't have to share every feeling you have, but it is important to share feelings when you or someone you know needs help. You don't have to solve every problem on your own. Sometimes you need help.

And if you do, talking about your feelings can be the first step toward getting it.

motional Intelligence and School

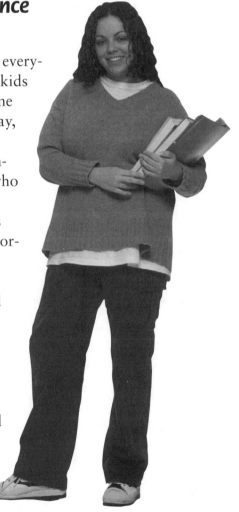

How's school? That's one subject everyone has an opinion about. Some kids love it. Some kids hate it. And some kids shrug their shoulders and say, "I guess it's okay."

Research done by social scientists who have studied students who "like school" versus those who "hate school," including students who drop out, gives us some important clues about school success. What they found is that students who enjoyed school the most, and who were more likely to feel good about themselves, were those who participated in clubs or events that the school offered outside of class. Why? Because extracurricular activities allowed these students to showcase other abilities. Some students may not be "book smart," but they are very smart or talented in other ways, ways that a paper and pencil test can't measure.

And even if you're a student who gets good grades, out-of-class activities can help you develop other skills and strengths. Extracurriculars also help you feel more connected to your school, and that's always a good thing.

motional Intelligence and the Job

The things you've been learning in this book—about being a healthy person in the way you feel and how you react to feelings—will apply doubly in a job setting. That's because at work you often will be under pressure to do a task and do it well. You also may have to do the task quickly, such as taking orders at a fast-food restaurant.

This is why it's important to seek jobs that allow you to do at least one of these things:

- Improve your skills
- Improve your knowledge
- Improve your leadership capabilities

Learning how to give your best effort and get along with a variety of people can help you succeed on the job—and maybe even get a pay raise!

motional Intelligence and Your Life

Being happy and successful depends on far more than being smart or good looking or rich or talented. Psychologists and other people who study human behavior have found that emotional well-being often matters more than any of those things—and they're not talking smack!

Something's missing in the success equation when we feel unmotivated, or when we can't get along with other people. Having talent without motivation equals less than a full life. Riches without inner peace equals less than a full life, and so on. So don't let anyone tell you that feelings aren't important; they are a key variable in your personal success equation.

Often we want to be successful, but we mess up. Then we decide to give up. We stop before we have a chance to succeed at anything. If at first you don't succeed, it might be because you didn't try at all. What are *you* going to do?

show what you know

1. *What does it mean to be a "team player"? Define it.*

_____

_____

_____

_____

_____

_____

2. *What does it mean to be a "leader"? Define it.*

_____

_____

_____

_____

_____

_____

3. *What does it mean to be a "positive influence"? Define it.*

_____

_____

_____

_____

_____

_____

keeping your journal

GET IN TOUCH WITH HOW YOU FEEL

1. This chapter describes three personal skills: being a team player, being a leader, and being a positive influence. How good are you at these three skills? Or are you not so good?

_____

_____

_____

_____

_____

_____

_____

_____

_____

2. In which area would you like to improve? How will you plan to do this? How might talking it through with some-one else help you develop your social skills?

_____

_____

_____

_____

_____

_____

_____

_____

_____

APPENDIX

your journal

E ach of the following journal pages has a quote or a question for you to think about. Use the quotes and related questions to guide your writing. Journaling allows you to see how your thoughts grow and change over time. You will also learn more about yourself as you continue in your journaling. Write about your thoughts, your daily life, your dreams for the future, or anything else you deem worthy.

Learn as though you would never be able to master it;
hold it as though you would be in fear of losing it.

—**CONFUCIUS** (551–479 BC), CHINESE ETHICAL TEACHER AND PHILOSOPHER

How can you teach other people what you have learned in this book?

_____

_____

_____

_____

_____

_____

_____

_____

_____

_____

_____

_____

_____

_____

_____

_____

_____

_____

_____

_____

_____

_____

_____

_____

Only those who risk going too far can possibly find out how far one can go.

—**T.S. ELIOT** (1888–1965), AMERICAN POET AND CRITIC

_____

_____

_____

_____

_____

_____

_____

_____

_____

_____

_____

_____

_____

_____

_____

_____

_____

_____

What does courage mean to you?

A capacity to change is indispensable. Equally indispensable is the capacity to hold fast to that which is good.

—**JOHN FOSTER DULLES** (1888–1959), AMERICAN LAWYER AND POLITICIAN

How can you change the world?

The best way to predict the future is to create it.

—**PETER F. DRUCKER** (1909–PRESENT), AMERICAN MANAGEMENT
CONSULTANT AND AUTHOR

How are today's actions related to your future?

An adventure is only an inconvenience rightly considered. An inconvenience is only an adventure wrongly considered.

—**G. K. CHESTERTON** (1874–1936), ENGLISH AUTHOR

_____

_____

_____

_____

_____

_____

_____

_____

_____

_____

_____

_____

_____

_____

_____

_____

_____

_____

_____

When was the last time you challenged yourself?

A man does not have to be an angel in order to be a saint.

—**ALBERT SCHWEITZER** (1875–1965), GERMAN HUMANITARIAN

Write briefly about someone you look up to and be sure to explain why.

Discipline is the soul of an army. It makes small numbers formidable; procures success to the weak, and esteem to all.

—GEORGE WASHINGTON (1732–1799), FIRST PRESIDENT OF THE UNITED STATES

Define discipline *in your own words.*

He who controls others may be powerful,

but he who has mastered himself is mightier still.

—LAO TZU (600–? BC), CHINESE PHILOSOPHER AND FOUNDER OF TAOISM

_____

_____

_____

_____

_____

_____

_____

_____

_____

_____

_____

_____

_____

_____

_____

_____

_____

_____

_____

In what ways can you delay gratification?

He that does good for good's sake seeks neither paradise nor reward, but he is sure of both in the end.

—WILLIAM PENN (1644–1718), ENGLISH RELIGIOUS LEADER, FOUNDER OF PENNSYLVANIA

_____

_____

_____

_____

_____

_____

_____

_____

_____

_____

_____

_____

_____

_____

_____

_____

_____

How can you reward yourself after working hard?

My mother said to me, "If you become a soldier, you'll be a general; if you become a monk, you'll end up as the pope." Instead, I became a painter and wound up as Picasso.

—**PABLO PICASSO** (1881–1973), SPANISH ARTIST

What is something you have to offer the world?

There is little that can withstand a man who can conquer himself.

—**LOUIS XIV** (1638–1715), KING OF FRANCE FROM 1643 TO 1715

What is your mission in life?

_____

_____

_____

_____

_____

_____

_____

_____

_____

_____

_____

_____

_____

_____

_____

_____

_____

_____

_____

_____

_____

_____

_____

_____

_____

_____

How do you know if your mission in life is finished?
If you're still alive, it isn't.

—**RICHARD BACH** (1936–PRESENT), AMERICAN AUTHOR

_____

_____

_____

_____

_____

_____

_____

_____

_____

_____

_____

_____

_____

_____

_____

_____

_____

_____

_____

_____

What is important about your mission in life?

To exist is to change, to change is to mature,
to mature is to go on creating oneself endlessly.

—**HENRI L. BERGSON** (1859–1941), FRENCH PHILOSOPHER

Describe your life in thirty years.

Many of life's failures are people who did not realize how close they were to success when they gave up.

—**THOMAS A. EDISON** (1847–1931), AMERICAN INVENTOR, ENTREPRENEUR, FOUNDER OF GENERAL ELECTRIC

How can you challenge yourself this year?

_____
_____
_____
_____
_____
_____
_____
_____
_____
_____
_____
_____
_____
_____
_____
_____
_____
_____
_____
_____
_____
_____
_____
_____

The little reed, bending to the force of the wind, soon stood upright again when the storm had passed over.

—**AESOP** (620–560 BC), GREEK FABULIST

_____

_____

_____

_____

_____

_____

_____

_____

_____

_____

_____

_____

_____

_____

_____

_____

_____

_____

_____

Write about the hardest thing you have ever had to deal with.

It is impossible for a man to begin to learn
what he thinks he knows.

—**EPICTETUS** (AD 55–135), GREEK PHILOSOPHER

What have you learned about yourself lately?

_____

_____

_____

_____

_____

_____

_____

_____

_____

_____

_____

_____

_____

_____

_____

_____

_____

_____

_____

_____

_____

_____

_____

_____

_____

_____

_____

_____

Nothing is more difficult, and therefore
more precious, than to be able to decide.

—**NAPOLEON BONAPARTE** (1769–1821), FRENCH GENERAL AND EMPEROR

Who can help you make good decisions about your future and why?

_____

_____

_____

_____

_____

_____

_____

_____

_____

_____

_____

_____

_____

_____

_____

_____

_____

_____

_____

_____

_____

_____

_____

Whether you think that you can, or that you can't,
you are usually right.

—**HENRY FORD** (1863–1947), MACHINIST, ENGINEER,
FOUNDER OF FORD MOTOR COMPANY

_____

_____

_____

_____

_____

_____

_____

_____

_____

_____

_____

_____

_____

_____

_____

_____

_____

_____

Why is it important to have positive role models?

_____
_____
_____
_____
_____
_____
_____
_____
_____
_____
_____
_____
_____
_____
_____
_____
_____
_____
_____
_____
_____
_____
_____
_____
_____

The block of granite which was an obstacle in the pathway of the weak becomes a stepping-stone in the pathway for the strong.

—**THOMAS CARLYLE** (1795–1881), SCOTTISH PHILOSOPHER AND AUTHOR

Do you believe that you can do anything *you want? Why or why not?*

_____

_____

_____

_____

_____

_____

_____

_____

_____

_____

_____

_____

_____

_____

_____

_____

_____

_____

_____

_____

_____

_____

_____

_____

We cannot solve problems with the same kind of thinking used when creating them.

—ALBERT EINSTEIN (1879–1955), FAMOUS SWISS-AMERICAN SCIENTIST

Write about a time when you became discouraged about a project or task. Why did you feel this way?

One of the signs of passing youth is the birth of a sense of fellowship with other human beings as we take our place among them.

—**VIRGINIA WOOLF** (1882–1941), ENGLISH MODERNIST, NOVELIST

What makes you unique?

A person's worth in this world is estimated according to the value they put on themselves.

JEAN DE LA BRUYÈRE (1645–1696), FRENCH WRITER

_____

_____

_____

_____

_____

_____

_____

_____

_____

_____

_____

_____

_____

_____

_____

_____

_____

_____

_____

_____

Write about a time when a public figure (pro athlete, actor, politician, etc.) lacked emotional intelligence. Did this change the way you felt about him or her?

It does not take much strength to do things,
but it requires great strength to decide what to do.

—**ELBERT HUBBARD** (1856–1915), AMERICAN AUTHOR AND PUBLISHER

_____
_____
_____
_____
_____
_____
_____
_____
_____
_____
_____
_____
_____
_____
_____
_____
_____
_____

Write about the most important decision you've ever made.

The artist is nothing without the gift,

but the gift is nothing without the work.

—EMILE ZOLA (1840–1902), FRENCH JOURNALIST AND NOVELIST

_____

_____

_____

_____

_____

_____

_____

_____

_____

_____

_____

_____

_____

_____

_____

_____

_____

_____

_____

_____

_____

In what ways can you improve your emotional intelligence?

How far you go in life depends on your being tender with the young, compassionate with the aged, sympathetic with the striving, and tolerant of the weak and strong. Because someday in your life you will have been all of these.

—**GEORGE WASHINGTON CARVER** (1861–1943), AMERICAN SCIENTIST, EDUCATOR, AND HUMANITARIAN

Do you consider your self emotionally intelligent? Why or why not?

_____

_____

_____

_____

_____

_____

_____

_____

_____

_____

_____

_____

_____

_____

_____

_____

_____

_____

_____

_____

_____

_____

The following books are available through Prentice Hall Publishers.
Visit www.prenhall.com (search by keywords "keys to").

The following books are available through LifeBound. Visit www.lifebound.com.

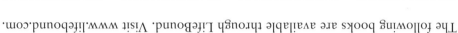